ROMAN ESKDALE

R.G. COLLINGWOOD,
M.A., F.S.A.

ROMAN ESKDALE

by

R. G. COLLINGWOOD, M.A., F.S.A.

Fellow of Pembroke College, Oxford, and Lecturer in Philosophy and Classical History in the University of Oxford, Member of the Council of the Society of Antiquaries, London, and Editor to the Cumberland and Westmorland Antiquarian and Archæological Society.

R. G. Collingwood

Robin George Collingwood was born on 22nd February 1889, in Cartmel, England. He was the son of author, artist, and academic, W. G. Collingwood.

Collingwood attended Rugby School before enrolling at University College, Oxford, where he received a congratulatory first class honours for reading Greats. He became a fellow of Pembroke College, Oxford, and remained there for 15 years until he was offered the post of Waynflete Professor of Metaphysical Philosophy at Magdalen College, Oxford. He was greatly influenced by the Italian Idealists Croce, Gentile, and Guido de Ruggiero. Another important influence was his father, a professor of fine art and a student of Ruskin.

Collingwood produced *The Principles of Art* in 1938, outlining the concept of art as being essentially expressions of emotion. He claimed that it was a necessary function of the human mind and considered it an important collaborative activity. He also published other works of philosophy, such as *Speculum Mentis* (1924), *An Essay on Philosophic Method* (1933), *An Essay on Metaphysics* (1940), and many more. In 1940, he published *The First Mate's Log,* an account of a sailing trip he undertook with some of his students in the Mediterranean.

Collingwood died at Coniston, Lancashire on January 1943, after a series of debilitating strokes.

CONTENTS.

Introduction
Eskdale before the Romans
The Coming of the Romans
The Roman Road in Eskdale
The Pottery and Tilery at Park House
Hardknot Castle
Hardknot Castle : Situation
Hardknot Castle : the Fort (defences)
Hardknot Castle : the Fort (internal buildings)
Hardknot Castle : the Bath-house
Hardknot Castle : the Parade-ground
Hardknot Castle : its History
The Roman Fort at Ravenglass
"Walls Castle" : the Roman Bath-house at Ravenglass
The History of Roman Ravenglass

ILLUSTRATIONS.

Hardknot Castle : plan of the fort and surroundings
Hardknot Castle : plan of the fort
Hardknot Castle : plan of the bath-house
Hardknot Castle :
    (a) the circular SUDATORIUM (b) the furnace of the baths, as they were when first excavated
Walls Castle : plan
Walls Castle : general view
Walls Castle : relieving arch over door
Walls Castle : niche

Introduction.

Of all the valleys of England there is none lovelier than Eskdale, from its wild beginning among the precipices of Scafell to its quiet ending in the land-locked harbour of Ravenglass. But its landscape, incomparable though it is, is not the only charm that it offers to visitors. More than most of the dales of Cumberland, it is rich in history, and can show ancient remains that might make it a place of pilgrimage even to people who cared nothing for scenery. Of these the chief are its two Roman forts, one on the mountain-side of Hardknot, the other at Ravenglass by the sea-shore.

This little guide-book is written to explain these forts, and the other Roman remains in Eskdale, to every visitor who wishes to know what they mean. It has been written and published with the permission of the Cumberland and Westmorland Antiquarian and Archæological Society, which visited these places in 1927 and ordered the writer to compile descriptions of them for the occasion. These descriptions, involving a fresh study of all the evidence, were found to lead to several new conclusions ; and the Society, after publishing them in its TRANSACTIONS, kindly allowed the material contained in them, and the illustrations accompanying them, to be used over again in the form of a guide-book.

Apart from the material derived from these papers in the Society's TRANSACTIONS, new series, vol. xxviii, this book depends chiefly on two sources: Mr. W. G. Collingwood's LAKE DISTRICT HISTORY, which every visitor to the district ought to read, and no one can read without delight and instruction; and the local studies of Miss Mary C. Fair, whose generous gifts of information and of her own beautiful photographs have been a constant help in the work whose results are described in these pages.

ROMAN ESKDALE.

ESKDALE BEFORE THE ROMANS

Before the Romans came, and even after they went away, no one lived, as men live now, along the bottom of Eskdale. In those days the valley-bottoms of these parts were full of timber, great or small, and marshy with standing water or stony with the leavings of flooded becks. At the head of Wastwater there is a little patch of ground which to-day still shows what all these valleys were once like : banks of shingle and hollows of swamp, all overgrown with scrubby little trees. The green fields that follow one another down Eskdale are no more of Nature's making than the stone dikes that divide them. They have been made by man ; and man did not begin to make them, stubbing bushes and draining swamps and embanking becks, until hundreds of years after the Romans left. The Northern Farmer, old style, who " stubbed Thurnaby waste " in Tennyson's poem, was of Anglo-Saxon or Scandinavian blood, the blood of a race which " mixed its labour with the land " and so, in the words of Locke, " put the greatest part of the value upon land, without which it would scarcely be worth anything." In Eskdale this work was done by descendants of those Norsemen who settled outside the mountain district in the tenth

ROMAN ESKDALE

century and, generation after generation, worked their way up the dales, until, by about the thirteenth century, the farms were disposed very much as we now know them.

Prehistoric man never set himself this task of reclaiming the valley-bottoms and using them for agriculture. Not that he was ignorant of agriculture; on the contrary, it was his staple livelihood as far back as we can trace him in these parts of the country; but he worked the soil where, poor though it was, it could be got at with less difficulty and worked without elaborate clearing and draining.

This state of things he found on the high ground that lies between the mountains and the valleys. These shelves of upland, too high to be encumbered with marsh and wood like the valleys, not high enough to be incapable of cultivation like the mountain-tops, are the places where we find all the prehistoric remains in the Lake District. Such remains are plentiful on either side of Eskdale. On the north are the Bronze Age circles of Burnmoor; burial-places of people who must have tilled the ground on the plateau between Eskdale and Wastdale, and hunted on the higher fells, perhaps a thousand years before Christ. One of them lost a flint arrow-head when hunting along the Wastwater Screes. South of Eskdale there is a vast collection of hut-circles at Barnscar, on the high shelf of land south-west of Devoke Water. "British Settlements" like these belong to the Early Iron Age, which, hereabouts, means the last few centuries B C. and the first few centuries A.D. The beehive huts at Barnscar were very likely inhabited for a good many generations before the Romans came, and during all the time the Romans were here.

ROMAN ESKDALE

Thus we get a fairly complete idea of Eskdale before the Romans. The sides and bottom of the valley uninhabited and covered with scrub ; the bottom marshy as well ; people living a rough and poor kind of life on the uplands, tilling their little fields and eking out their produce by keeping a few cattle and sheep and hunting on the mountains and in the forests.

THE COMING OF THE ROMANS

A British chief, taken to Rome as a captive, asked why the men who possessed so splendid a city should have envied him his poor dwelling. We need not ask here what it was that brought the Romans to Britain, but we must certainly ask what brought them to Eskdale.

South-eastern and central England, invaded in A.D. 43, were quickly overrun by Roman armies. But Wales and the mountainous north were another matter. It was not until the governorship of the great Julius Agricola (77-84) that the conquest of Wales was finished and that of the north seriously taken in hand. In 78, the last resistance in Wales crushed, Agricola turned northward and began the systematic conquest of Brigantia—all England between the Humber and the Tyne—which had been rapidly overrun, some years earlier, by Petilius Cerialis.

Antiquaries used to believe that they could establish Agricola's precise line of march, and took sides in favour of this route or that. To-day we are content with less; but we demand a higher standard of proof. We know that there were then, as there are now, two ways to the north: one by Cheshire and Lancashire to the Lune valley and so to Penrith

ROMAN ESKDALE

and Carlisle, the other by the Vale of York to the Tyne. We may be sure that Agricola's armies used both these routes, and built roads and forts along them; for we find relics that can be dated to his lifetime when we dig at sites along these lines. At one such site, Lancaster, a branch road leaves the main Carlisle road and bends off westwards. It goes to Watercrook, just south of Kendal, where there is a Roman fort in an elbow of the river Kent. Thence it goes to Ambleside, where there is another, down by the water's edge at the head of Windermere. Thence it strikes up Little Langdale, over Wrynose, past Cockley Beck, over Hardknot Pass, and down Eskdale to the sea at Ravenglass.

When and why did the Romans build this road?

First of all, when? The answer is given by digging done some years ago at Ambleside. The fort whose stone foundations are still visible in Borrans Field, owned by the National Trust and open to the public, dates from the second century A.D.; but underneath these foundations were discovered the remains of an earlier Roman fort, with earthern ramparts and wooden buildings, and the things found in it showed that it had been built late in the first century, no doubt in the time of Agricola. Now the fort cannot have been earlier than the road; and the road cannot have stopped short at Ambleside; therefore it is safe to argue that Agricola was responsible for the whole of this branch-line from Lancaster through the mountains to Eskdale and the sea.

Roman Eskdale, then, is Agricola's work. But why was this work done?

ROMAN ESKDALE

The branch-road from Lancaster to the sea cannot be explained by the necessity of keeping touch between the army and the fleet. That could be secured at Lancaster and again at Carlisle ; and nothing in that respect could be gained by driving a road through the Lake District. Nor can it be explained by any fancied necessity of conquering or patrolling the Lake District mountains. The central mountains were practically uninhabited, and what population there was lived on the uplands on the edge of the mountain region. Agricola's road does not touch these inhabited regions, and was plainly never designed to keep their inhabitants under control. In short, we must look rather carefully at the facts if we are to explain the motives which led to the construction of the Lancaster-Ambleside-Ravenglass road.

At no time in history has there ever been any permanent reason for a road over Wrynose and Hardknot. The permanent economic needs of the country do not require it, and never did. Permanent military considerations do not require it, and never did. Such a road could be of no value to West Cumberland, whose natural land communications are with Carlisle and Penrith, or to South Cumberland, which is easily accessible from Broughton-in-Furness. For a while, in the nineteenth century, a carriage-road existed along this line in modern times ; but it was allowed to fall into disrepair simply because it was not worth keeping up. The insignificant traffic which it might carry could not justify the cost of repairing it. The project of a new road on the same line would never have appeared but for the system under which main roads are heavily subsidised by the State, which

ROMAN ESKDALE

makes it possible in certain circumstances to gain trifling local advantages by a large expenditure of other people's money.

The reason for Agricola's road between Lancaster and Ravenglass was a purely temporary reason. Tacitus, in his Life of Agricola, tells us that in the year 81 Agricola " placed troops in that part of Britain which faces Ireland, with a view to hope [of invading that country] rather than through fear [or Irish raids] ; because Ireland, lying midway between Britain and Spain, and within easy reach of the Gaulish sea, would unite the most flourishing regions of the Empire with great advantage to each " (*eamque partem Britanniae quae Hiberniam aspicit copiis instruxit, in spem magis quam ob formidinem, si quidem Hibernia medio inter Britanniam et Hispaniam sita et Gallico mari opportuna valentissimam partem imperii magnis in vicem usibus miscuerit*).

Agricola's geography may have been a little shaky, but he was right in thinking that prehistoric Ireland was a country in regular communication with Spain, and that its possession would, together with that of Scotland, round off and secure the Roman Empire in the west of Europe. And this passage tells us that he actually chose a place on the western coast of Britain from which an invasion of Ireland might be launched.

Where was this place ? A careful study of all the known Roman sites on the western coast of Britain seems to prove that there is only one which can seriously claim to be Agricola's choice. It must be on a first-rate harbour ; it must face Ireland ; it must have first-century Roman remains ; and it must

ROMAN ESKDALE

be connected with the army headquarters at York or Chester by a direct road. Ravenglass fulfils all these conditions. The harbour is now silted up, but it must have been a magnificent one in Agricola's time ; and the fort lies right by the water's edge as if to impress on every visitor the connexion between the fort and the harbour. On fine days the Isle of Man is visible from the shore, and in very clear weather you see the Mourne Mountains from the hills a little way inland, even at times from the shore itself. The road to Ravenglass, we have seen, dates from Agricola, and therefore presumably the fort does too. And the road gives direct communication with Chester, Agricola's chief army-base.

The whole situation is now clear and intelligible. The Eskdale road is a purely strategic road, leading to Ravenglass ; and the reason why a road is needed is that Ravenglass has been chosen as a naval base for the projected campaign against Ireland. Apart from this project, there was nothing to bring Agricola into the Lake District at all. His main road up the Lune valley could easily be secured against native raids on its left flank by an occasional demonstration on the part of the garrisons placed in its forts ; he could leave the Lake District alone, just as he left Galloway alone.

Roman Eskdale, then, is a by-product of a scheme that never came off. But the Romans were tenacious people. Having established a fort at Ravenglass, they did not like to abandon it. So they kept it up ; and, as we shall see, they even reinforced it by building Hardknot Castle, some years later, to make it a little less isolated, a little less remote from its nearest neighbour. Later, when Hadrian had built his great wall across England,

ROMAN ESKDALE

Hardknot was abandoned, but Ravenglass still remained. It was a useful port of call for coastwise shipping, and it acted as a kind of remote outpost far away on the left wing of the Wall. But the road, once Hardknot was given up, can have been very little used. At any rate, no milestones have ever been found on it ; and since old milestones were thrown away and new ones put up whenever a road was extensively repaired, the number of milestones found along the line of a road gives a hint of the amount of work that was done on it.

THE ROMAN ROAD IN ESKDALE

If their road had been of real permanent value to the Romans, they would have kept it in repair ; and if they had kept it in repair, it would have been fairly easy to trace. But, even on ground that has never been cultivated, it is a curiously elusive road ; as contrasted with other mountain roads of the Roman period, the difficulty of tracing it is quite extraordinary. This difficulty of course increases when we come down to cultivated ground intersected by all manner of medieval and modern tracks. Therefore everything that can be said about the Roman road in Eskdale must be said with caution and accepted as purely tentative.

Plainly, the road must have entered the valley at Hardknot pass, run down past Hardknot Castle into the valley, and so to Ravenglass. The two forts, Hardknot and Ravenglass, are fixed points, and we may begin—remembering the Roman engineers' passion for a bee-line—by ruling a line on the map to join them. This line will not quite do, because it takes us over a formidable crag opposite Eskdale Green. But if we divert the line

ROMAN ESKDALE

so as to clear this crag, we find it following a not impossible track. At first it runs down the left bank of the Esk, to Spothow and Low Birker ; then it leaves Dalegarth Hall on the right and climbs over a pass nearly 500 feet high, coming down into the valley again at Field Head ; thence it runs down the dale, crossing the Esk somewhere, and so by Muncaster Castle to Ravenglass.

But this is a merely theoretical line ; and it would be very definitely improved if instead of climbing the pass to the left of Dalegarth Hall it bore to the right, keeping closer to the river and crossing it at Forge House. Thence it could proceed in a fairly straight line to Ravenglass without further obstacles.

Such is the train of thought which we imagine to pass in the mind of a Roman engineer laying out a road from Hardknot pass to Ravenglass harbour. We can now turn to the ground itself, and see whether any visible relics confirm or overthrow our hypothesis.

In the first place, there is a Roman site two-thirds of the way from Hardknot to Ravenglass. This is a pottery and tilery, situated a mile S.S.W. of Eskdale Green, at Park House. In the absence of thorough excavation we cannot as yet say much about its history, but there is no doubt of its character, and it was certainly working when Hardknot Castle was built, about A.D. 100. We cannot doubt that it lay on the line of road, or quite close to it. And it lies on what is still a road, running N.E. and S.W. and connecting Muncaster with Eskdale Green.

ROMAN ESKDALE

In the second place, a careful study of the ground had been made by an Eskdale archæologist, Miss Mary C. Fair, who has brought to light many stretches and fragments of old roads which provide a clue to the line probably taken by the Roman engineers. Miss Fair's view of the Roman road is that it branches off to the left from the modern road at the foot of Hardknot pass, travelling in a straight line still marked by gateways in the modern field-walls, and so by a still visible causeway to the demolished farm-house, Spothow. Hence it went, she thinks, in a straight line to Low Birker, and then through Underbank Wood to a ford in Stanley Gill Beck and so to Dalegarth Hall. Passing just south of the Hall it follows a line marked by stiles in the walls, and after passing the ruined farm of Red Brow crosses the Esk north-west of Forge House, at a place where in dry weather may be seen some indications of a made ford. It then crosses Mere Beck and skirts a swampy hollow north of Muncaster Head farm, where Miss Fair found it by excavation 9 feet wide and solidly constructed with good kerb-stones. It comes to a hillock locally known as Bull Kop, 300 yards north-west of Muncaster Head; and passing round the north side of the summit it picks its way between patches of soft ground and slopes down to join the private drive (that is to say, the road that runs by Muncaster Head and High Eskholme) 700 yards W.S.W. of Muncaster Head and 300 yards N.E. of Park House. It now follows the private drive for just over a mile, to a point 200 yards beyond High Eskholme. Here it has been thought to leave the private drive and slant up the side of Muncaster Fell to a point 500 feet above the sea, just below the summit of Chapel Hill, and thence down to Branken Wall and Home Farm and so to

ROMAN ESKDALE

the fort. But Miss Fair now thinks that it can be traced on a line passing between Muncaster Castle and Muncaster Church, which would imply that it ran along low ground from High Eskholme to near Muncaster Castle and thence to the Ravenglass fort without going out of its way to climb Muncaster Fell. On general grounds of probability this is far more satisfactory.

Miss Fair's line, as thus defined, follows the track which a Roman engineer would naturally take; it is based on detailed local study ; and it has been verified at several points by the discovery of odd roads closely resembling Roman roads in construction. Miss Fair's theory, therefore, holds the field and any reader who can improve on it is welcome to do so.

THE POTTERY AND TILERY AT PARK HOUSE

Three miles north-west of Ravenglass is the now deserted farm of Park House, where, as I have already said, there are the remains of a Roman pottery and tilery. Kilns of this kind have been found in many parts of England. For the most part they are very simply constructed. A cavity in the ground forms the furnace. Over this is a flat roof solidly made of clay, with holes in it. On this roof the pottery was stacked, and a dome of clay was built over it. The furnace was then lit, being fed and tended through a flue from a second pit acting as stoke-hole. The hot gases rose from the furnace into the domed superstructure, where they fired the pottery and escaped through a vent in the dome. This dome had to be rebuilt every time the kiln was used.

ROMAN ESKDALE

Some time about 1890 the establishment at Park House was dug, but apparently—as was often the case at that time—without expert advice and without keeping any record of what was found ; the result was, of course, that the kilns were badly damaged and no one was any the wiser. Recently Miss Fair has examined the site and partially re-excavated it, and what follows is the result of her investigations.

There seem to have been at least two kilns, besides a pit which may have been the source from which the Romans got their clay, and a mound which may be the ruins of the house in which they lived. The northernmost kiln is visible as an underground chamber, whose roof is at ground-level and is pierced by a hole through which the interior of the chamber can be seen. This chamber is built partly of local granite, covered with cement, and partly of good Roman tiles. Its roof is supported by square pillars of Roman tiles, like the pillars supporting the floor of a Roman house heated with hypocausts. These pillars can be seen through the hole in the roof, and so can the end of a flue entering the chamber at one side.

The second kiln, south-east of the first, has been examined by Miss Fair and found to consist of substantial brickwork made of tiles about half an inch thick. In the middle was a chamber whose roof was supported on brick pillars, and under this a second chamber with brick pillars exactly underneath those of the upper chamber. The lower chamber was no doubt the furnace ; the upper must have been the firing-chamber, in this case a permanent structure, not a mere temporary dome of clay.

ROMAN ESKDALE

During these excavations a great quantity of tiles and bricks of various shapes and sizes were found, and numerous fragments of pottery showing the kinds of ware made at the establishment. Pending further diggings, we cannot say when these kilns were first built and how long they continued at work ; but there can be little doubt that they produced the large tiles or bricks used in the fort at Hardknot and a good deal of the pottery found there. This means that they were working at least from A.D. 100 to A.D. 130. Their unusually massive and expensive construction makes them interesting as an example of an official military pottery and tilery, a far more ambitious and elaborate establishment than the simple kilns of private potters in Roman Britain.

HARDKNOT CASTLE

The great Elizabethan antiquary, William Camden, heard that at the head of Eskdale was " Hard-Knot, an high steepe mountain, in the top whereof were discovered of late huge stones and foundations of a castle, not without great wonder, considering that it is so steepe and upright that one can hardly ascend up to it." It was not until two hundred years later that the first plan of the site was made and the first description written. At the beginning of the nineteenth century people recognised it as a Roman fort—or " camp," as they called it, not distinguishing between a camp, which was a slight temporary earthwork to shelter the tents of a marching army, and a fort, a permanent structure garrisoned by a small body of troops—and in 1820 Wordsworth wrote of

...that lone camp on Hardknot's height
Whose guardians bent the knee to Jove and Mars.

ROMAN ESKDALE

During the course of the century a fragment of a Roman inscription, too mutilated to be intelligible, came to light ; and finally, in 1889-1892, the Cumberland and Westmorland Antiquarian and Archæological Society dug the place with commendable care and thoroughness. It is on these diggings that we rely for all our knowledge of the fort. They were carried out at a time when scientific archæology was in its infancy ; this was one of the first Roman forts to be dug in this country ; and the people who dug it were not able to interpret the history of the site by reference to the objects found in it, because the principles on which that interpretation depends had not yet been discovered. But they made and published careful descriptions and beautiful plans of the buildings unearthed, and they laid aside the objects they found, carefully packed in parcels, so that thirty years later these could be examined in the light of modern knowledge and the history of the fort deciphered. In 1927, when the Cumberland and Westmorland Antiquarian Society visited the site, it was at last possible to put forward a complete historical account of the Roman occupation ; and it is on that account, as published in the Society's TRANSACTIONS for 1928, that this description, by kind permission of the Society, is based.

HARDKNOT CASTLE : SITUATION

The fort lies about 800 feet above sea-level, on a spur that projects south-westward from the mountain-mass of Hardknot. It is about 9 miles from Ravenglass and 10 or 11 from Ambleside, these being the nearest Roman forts. The spur on which the fort is built juts out boldly into the valley,

HARDKNOT CASTLE: Plan of the Fort and Surroundings

ROMAN ESKDALE

bounded on one side by Hardknot Gill and on the other by precipitous crags overlooking Butterilket. Its summit is about 300 yards broad and 600 yards long ; this forms a patch of ground about 30 acres in extent, sloping towards the south and broken by numerous rounded hummocks of living rock, between which the soil is for the most part hard and gravelly. The whole site is naturally well drained, and not too rough to be built upon, nor too high above the sea to be lived upon ; for the warm sea winds prevent snow from ever lying long, even on the summit of the pass, 500 feet above.

The fort commands a splendid view. To the visitor who cares for magnificence of scenery, the sudden revelation of the Scafell range, as he reaches the edge of the spur and looks over the precipices and the valley below him at the mountains beyond, is an unforgettable experience. At the same time, turning westward, he can see clear down the valley to the Irish Sea ; and when the fort was being excavated the bell-tent pitched on the site was visible from the sea-shore. " Certainly," wrote Chancellor Ferguson, " the castle, with its walls and towers, would be visible [from the sea] ; and, to the rude natives, it must have looked an enchanted fortress in the air, the work of superhuman powers rather than of mere men. But I expect the rude natives had to carry up the stone."

Ravenglass harbour is not in sight, but it would have been an easy matter to keep a system of signals going—such a system as we know the Romans used, by flags, semaphores and fire signals—by means of a single intermediate post on Muncaster Fell. And eastward there is a clear view to the summit of the

ROMAN ESKDALE

pass. With a station there and another on the top of Wrynose, signals could be sent in a few minutes between Hardknot Castle and Ambleside.

The tactical situation of the fort is strong. On the north-west it is almost unapproachable by reason of the crags that overhang Butterilket ; on the south-west, the deep cleft of Hardknot Gill can only be crossed at a few points. Anyone attacking the fort must approach it along the line of the road, either from the pass or from the valley ; in either case, under observation from the fort and obliged to make the final assault awkwardly uphill. Modern artillery could knock the fort to pieces from the neighbouring mountain-tops ; but the catapults and ballistae of the Romans, even if the British tribes had possessed them, could hardly reach it from the upper slopes of Hardknot mountain.

HARDKNOT CASTLE : THE FORT (DEFENCES)

An ordinary Roman fort is a square or rectangular enclosure, with rounded corners and a gateway in each side ; it is defended by an earth rampart, or, more often, by one of earth and stone—stone wall with an earth bank piled against its inner side—and a ditch, single or more often double, all round.

Hardknot Castle is true to type in all essential respects. It is almost exactly square, measuring 375 feet each way ; its rounded corners face the cardinal points of the compass ; and its area inside the stone walls is just over 3 acres. When allowance has been made for the earth bank, the effective area may be estimated at 2.50 to 2.75 acres. In size and shape, it falls into a well-known series of forts belonging to the late first and early second centuries

ROMAN ESKDALE

A.D, designed to house a garrison of 500 men, a cohort of the rough auxiliary troops that the Romans levied, not, like the legions, from among civilised Roman citizens, but from the barbarian tribes on the frontiers of the Empire.

The stone rampart wall of Hardknot is to-day easily traced all round its circuit, where the excavators of 1892 cleared it of debris and left both inner and outer faces exposed to view. In nearly forty years the weather has damaged it, but it is still possible to see that the outer face is roughly coursed and the inner built in a haphazard fashion, showing that it was not meant to stand free but was concealed and supported by the earth bank which rested against it. This earth bank, and not the stone wall, was the real rampart of the fort. The stone wall was developed out of the wooden revetment and breastwork which was used to increase the height of an earthern rampart and to shelter its defenders. In the period when Hardknot was built, wood had been replaced by stone, but the function of the stonework was the same as that of the earlier timber structures. We must, therefore, think of the Roman soldiers at Hardknot manning the top of such an earth bank when a sudden attack threatened, and sheltering behind the battlements which crowned the stone parapet.

In each side was a gateway ; and the remains of these are still visible. The fort gate, called PORTA PRAETORIA, faces downhill towards the road. It was a double gate, 22 ft. 4 in. wide, which still shows, lying in its centre, a sandstone block remaining from the masonry pier that once divided the two openings. Each opening would be about 8 feet 6 inches wide, and would be closed by double doors

ROMAN ESKDALE

turning in the ordinary Roman fashion on hinges made by fitting iron pivots, at top and bottom, into cup-shaped holes in blocks of stone. One of these pivot-stones was found by the excavators at Hardknot, lying in its original place at the north side of the south-west gateway. The openings were arched, the arches and piers being made of red sandstone brought from the Gosforth neighbourhood, while the rest of the masonry was of rough, intractable mountain stone. The two side gates—the PORTA PRINCIPALIS DEXTRA to south-west and PORTA PRINCIPALIS SINISTRA to north-east—were very like the front gate, but a trifle smaller; here again, remains of the central piers still exist. The back gate, PORTA DECUMANA, is a single opening about 10 feet wide; but, allowing for the projection of the sandstone jambs, its original width must have been about the same as that of the openings of the front gate.

Why did the Roman builders provide so many gateways? The reason is to be found in tradition. A Roman fort was not so much a place inside which you were safe, as a place where soldiers lived, who had been trained to fight hand to hand in the open. The charge of infantry arranged in open order and armed with a short stabbing-sword was the tactical basis of all Roman military success. Rome did not conquer the world by fighting from behind walls. Therefore, when she took to building permanent forts for her frontier garrison troops, she was careful to provide them with broad gateways on every side, so that the garrison might get out with all possible speed and attack instead of waiting to be attacked. So firmly did she hold to this principle, that she even built gateways where no troops were likely ever to

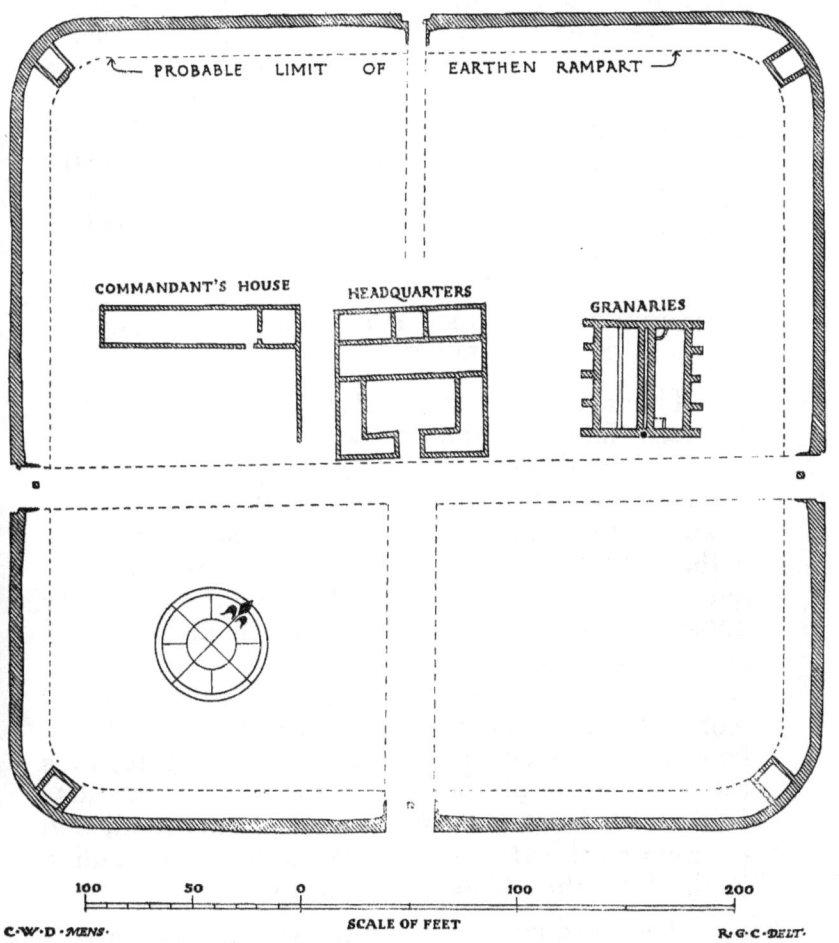

HARDKNOT CASTLE: Plan of the Fort

ROMAN ESKDALE

The fort, like all Roman forts, is surrounded by a ditch; but the ground is so rough and so rocky that a ditch is not required everywhere. It is most conspicuous where it runs round the northern angle, and here it is a rather impressive thing, cut as it is some 30 feet wide in the living rock. By the north-east gate, too, and at the eastern angle, it is well developed. Here and there along the north-east or uphill side of the fort a second ditch can be seen, also cut in the rock, and distant 80-100 feet from the fort.

HARDKNOT CASTLE : THE FORT (INTERNAL BUILDINGS)

The internal buildings of a Roman fort are laid out according to definite rules. Draw a line joining the centres of the front and back gates: Roman surveyors called that line the DECUMANUS MAXIMUS. Draw another, joining the centres of side gates: that is the KARDO MAXIMUS. At the point where these lines intersect, the surveyor set up his theodolite, or GROMA; and from this point the whole plan was laid out. The KARDO MAXIMUS becomes a road running right across the fort from side to side, the VIA PRINCIPALIS. Along the DECUMANUS MAXIMUS, from where the GROMA stands to the front gate, runs the chief road of the fort, the VIA PRAETORIA. Facing the front gate at the end of this road, and opening on the VIA PRINCIPALIS, is the chief building in the fort, the official headquarters.

The headquarters building at Hardknot is very simple in plan. Its gateway leads into a courtyard about 40 feet wide by 25 deep, surrounded on three sides by what was probably a colonnade or open cloister with a lean-to roof. On the fourth side was

ROMAN ESKDALE

a hall, or court—there is some doubt whether it was roofed over or not—65 feet long by 15 feet wide ; and beyond this was a range of rooms serving as the offices of the regiment. The central room was the regimental chapel, in which the standards were kept and sacrifice was offered to the gods of the Army and the Empire. Some sacred object, altar or statue, stood in the front courtyard, on the left side as you came in.

This building, though its foundations, as the visitor may still see, are of stone, was probably built of wood ; for the stone foundations are only 2 feet wide and seem too slight to have carried a solid stone building. It had glazed windows and was roofed and perhaps floored with tiles ; the chapel may have been roofed with lead. In one place there seems to have been a forge for the repair of weapons; in another, a pile of small pebbles, ammunition for slingers, was found.

North-east of the headquarters building is the granary, or rather granaries, for it is a twin block consisting of two buildings each 54 feet long by about 22 feet wide. The Roman army made its staple diet of bread ; and every fort had a granary capable of holding enough wheat to feed the garrison for a year. Now a ton of wheat occupies nearly a cubic yard and a half, and will feed three men for a year. A cohort of 500 men therefore requires 233, or say 250, cubic yards of space for its year's wheat-supply. The granaries at Hardknot would hold this without any difficulty. Indeed, if, as seems possible, the western granary was used for storing wheat, while the eastern was used for drying it in kilns, the required quantity could be kept by piling wheat 8 feet deep in the western granary alone.

ROMAN ESKDALE

The importance of the food-supply justified exceptional care in the building of the granary. It would never do to let the wheat spoil by getting damp, or to allow a sniper, shooting fire-arrows or hot clay sling bullets, to burn the granary down. Therefore the granary is by far the strongest building in the fort. Its walls are $3\frac{1}{2}$ feet thick, and surrounded by massive buttresses, showing that it was built in stone its full height and carried a heavy stone roof. Its floor was raised on sleeper-walls so as to be secure against damp, and often (though not at Hardknot) we find narrow windows low down in the walls, to ventilate the space beneath the raised floor. These, like many other features throwing light on Hardknot, can be seen in the neighbouring fort at Ambleside.

At Hardknot, there is a single sleeper-wall running from end to end of the granary, showing how the floor was raised by laying it on transverse joists. The excavators found that the walls of this granary had been plastered internally, to make them smooth and dry. In the eastern granary they found stone structures, which may have been kilns, in two corners, and no proof that there had ever been a raised floor. The western granary had a door at its south end, the other at its north.

On the other side of the headquarters building, one would expect to find the commanding officer's house. This was generally a courtyard house—a rectangular block with a courtyard in the middle, a veranda or colonnade all round that, and rooms opening off the veranda. Some part of such a house was found and excavated at Hardknot. The whole house must have measured about 95 by 60 feet ; the only rooms excavated were the range at

ROMAN ESKDALE

the back, consisting of one small room and one very long narrow room which must have been subdivided with wooden partitions. The parts excavated and shown on the plan have stone foundations, probably, like the headquarters building, with a wooden superstructure; the rest of the house was probably altogether built of wood. The whole house had been burnt down at some time, perhaps twice in the course of its history, as traces of repairs or reconstruction were found.

Various objects discovered in the commandant's house show the kind of life that was lived there. The pottery included the bright-red glazed "Samian" ware which served the purposes of our dining-room china, and other finds were a glass bowl and a leaden weight. There seemed to have been a hypocaust, and some of the floors were of tiles; the roof was apparently made of thin sandstone slabs.

These three buildings complete the central range, stretching from side to side of the fort and opening off the VIA PRINCIPALIS. It remains to account for the barracks where the troops lived, and for various other buildings such as workshops, stores, etc. These stood in the two remaining strips, the PRAETENTURA, or front strip, and the RETENTURA, or back strip. The PRAETENTURA is the larger of the two, and would easily hold six barrack-blocks, each about 120 feet long by 30 feet broad, running parallel to the VIA PRINCIPALIS. These would house the entire garrison, for a cohort of nominally 500 men was actually made up of six "centuries" of 80 men each—480 in all. This leaves the RETENTURA available for various buildings of other kinds.

ROMAN ESKDALE

As hardly any digging has been done in the PRAETENTURA and very little in the RETENTURA, the arrangement suggested is merely guesswork. But it is based on what we know of other forts like Hardknot; and it is confirmed by excavation to this extent, that some digging was carried out in the north-eastern part of the RETENTURA, and the remains of a heated building, if not two heated buildings, discovered. Now the barracks would certainly not be heated, and therefore this part of the RETENTURA, at any rate, did not contain barracks. One might perhaps imagine the heated building to have been the regimental hospital.

HARDKNOT CASTLE : THE BATH-HOUSE

Every Roman took his daily bath before dinner. The sterner moralists disapproved of the habit, holding that such luxury enfeebled body and mind; but their disapproval did not prevent anyone, even the moralists themselves, from continuing to bathe. The Roman bath was what we call a " Turkish " bath. By using that name we bear unconscious witness to the fact that, in the East, Roman customs survived the downfall of Roman rule and civilisation in the West. The Anglo-Saxons did not learn to bathe in Roman fashion; the Turks did.

A large Roman bathing-establishment is a very complicated thing; but reduced to its lowest terms, it consists of three rooms : one cold, one warm, and one hot. You go into the cold room (FRIGIDARIUM) and take off your clothes; then you go into the warm room (TEPIDARIUM) and get thoroughly warmed; then you go on into the hot room (CALDARIUM) where you perspire freely and are shampooed and rubbed down; then back into the TEPIDARIUM, and then

ROMAN ESKDALE

back to the FRIGIDARIUM where you have a cold plunge, and dress yourself if somebody has not stolen your clothes in the meantime—a misadventure corresponding, in Latin literature, to losing your overcoat in a modern restaurant, and certainly more trying to the sufferer.

Here at Hardknot we see the simplest type of Roman bath. It is a simple oblong building 66 feet long and 20 feet 6 inches wide, divided into three rooms. At the south is the hot room, heated by a furnace projecting from its south wall. This furnace

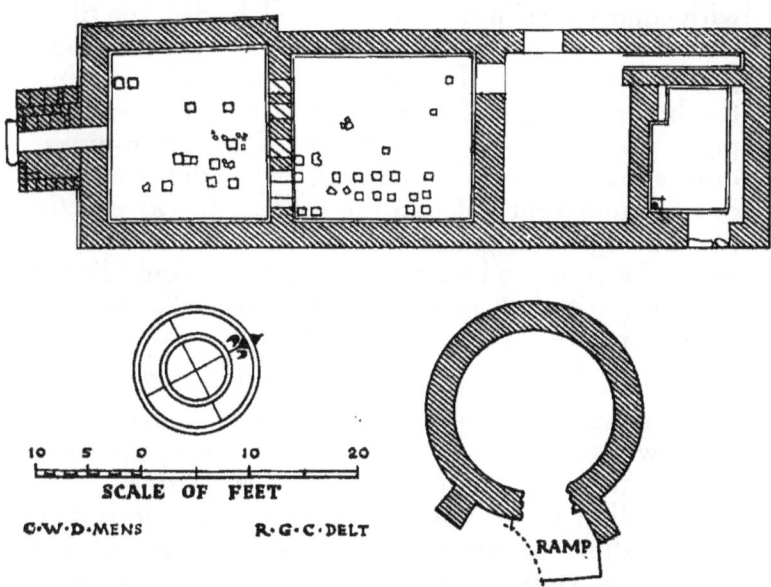

SCALE OF FEET

C·W·D·MENS   R·G·C·DELT   RAMP

was a handsome structure solidly built of large flat bricks, and when first found was complete up to well above the floor of the main flue; but, being left open for the public to see, it has been wantonly smashed to pieces by idle and mischievous loafers whose interest in ancient things goes to the length of destroying them. The mass of brickwork, 9 feet 2 in. wide and 6 ft. 6in. long, served to support a tank in which bath-water for use in the hot room was heated. Underneath the tank, the main flue led into the hypocaust-chamber beneath the floor of the hot room ; and when they had parted with their first heat the gases passed through large openings into the hypocaust chamber of the warm room, so that one furnace did the work of the whole establishment.

A hypocaust did not work by heating the floor of the room. Indeed, the floors were made so thick, with concrete reinforced by stone slabs or large tiles, that their surface can never have become more than pleasantly warm. The room was heated by leading the hot gases out of the hypocaust up the walls in pipes made of box-tiles—things like drain-pipes, only square, instead of round, in section—and so out through vent-holes in the walls. It was exactly like having radiators built into the walls ; and if you wanted a room to be extremely hot you could line it all round with hot-air pipes, so that its walls radiated heat from every part of themselves.

The hot room was 16 feet by 15 ft. 7in., and when it was excavated it contained a ruined hypocaust whose pillars, supporting the floor above, were made partly of brick and partly of sandstone. The west wall of this room is out of line with the rest of the building ; it has evidently been damaged and rebuilt in Roman times, and rebuilt, as often happened, in a careless or incompetent way. This is because a fort like Hardknot was originally built by the skilled professional architects and masons of the legions, but garrisoned by barbarian auxiliaries ; and if repairs were wanted, presumably the auxil-

ROMAN ESKDALE

iaries had to make what they could of the job for themselves. If they burnt their bath-house down they could not expect the legionary builders to come from York or Chester to rebuild it.

The warm room was 17 ft. 5 in. by 15 ft. 9 in. Its walls were found to be rendered in red cement, and it had a concrete floor resting on large slates supported by an offset in the wall and by brick and stone pillars, which stood on a second concrete floor. This hypocaust, when found, was in a fair state of preservation, but it is now completely ruined.

The cold room (23 ft. by 15 ft. 9 in.) is larger than the others because it has to contain the cold plunge-bath, which measures 11 ft. by 7 ft. 10 in. internally and consists of a masonry tank lined with waterproof cement containing pounded brick, and approached by a flight of steps leading down into its S.W. corner. At the S.E. corner was the opening of the waste-pipe, a lead pipe passing through a rock-cut trench. The rest of the cold room had a gravel floor, and in one place there was a stone base for an altar. Bath-houses were under the protection of the goddess Fortune, no doubt because they were the garrison's chief place of recreation, and recreation took the form of gambling. Consequently there seems always to have been an altar to Fortune in the entrance-hall or cold room, where men intending to gamble could solicit the favour of the goddess before getting to work.

There are two doors leading into the cold room from outside the building—one on the west, the other on the east. This is the stranger because the east door opens directly into the cold bath—an unintelligible arrangement. The explanation is

ROMAN ESKDALE

that the cold bath was at some time reduced in size by cutting off its eastern end. When that was done, the east door opened not into the cold bath but upon a platform perhaps five or six feet wide with the cold bath beyond it. Probably this alteration was made in order to make it possible to close up the west door and open out the east door to give easier communication with the round building to which we must now turn.

Many bath-houses of the late first and early second centuries include a round building separate from the main block, or a round room enclosed within it. This can be identified as the SUDATORIUM or LACONICUM, the " sweating-room " or " Spartan room," which was a specially hot room with a furnace of its own. It was roofed with a dome having an opening in the middle for ventilation, and its heat could be controlled by means of a brazen shutter hung on chains from this opening. The SUDATORIUM was entered either from the cold room or from a separate entrance-hall or courtyard, or, as here, from the open air outside the main building.

The Hardknot SUDATORIUM is 15 feet across internally. Its walls are well and solidly built, no doubt because they had to carry a dome. Its doorway faces downhill and was approached by a sloping pavement or ramp; there were two buttresses on this downhill side of the building, where the weight of the roof no doubt most needed support. The excavators found no hypocaust and no furnace; but they found a mass of broken bricks and flue-tiles under the floor, which made it obvious that there had once been a hypocaust and that it had been demolished at some time when the building was no

HARDKNOT CASTLE

(a) The Circular Sudatorium

(b) The Furnace of the Baths, as they were when first excavated

Photos by W. L. Fletcher.

ROMAN ESKDALE

longer needed for its original purpose. The inside of the walls had been rendered in pink cement.

The water-supply for the baths was evidently derived from the little stream which flows past them. About 30 feet away from the baths, this stream forms a pond, artificially made by damming its course. Whether the water was led in a pipe or brought as required in buckets, we do not know.

HARDKNOT CASTLE : THE PARADE GROUND

The most remarkable feature at Hardknot is the " bowling green," as it is locally called ; an artificially levelled patch of ground 100 yards by 150, or a trifle over 3 acres in extent, lying 250 yards away from the fort. It is roughly rectangular, and has been made with considerable labour by cutting away the ground on the north and embanking it on the south, so as to give a uniform slope of about 1 in 15. How well it has been designed and made, is evident from the fact that even to-day the whole area is firm and dry, undamaged by the weather and covered with good turf.

This levelled area is approached by a well-made road leading from the PORTA PRINCIPALIS SINISTRA of the fort ; and in the middle of its north-west side it is commanded by a mound, largely artificial, and made of piled stones.

The " bowling-green " can hardly be anything else than the parade-ground of the fort. It is obvious that every Roman fort must have had a place where the garrison could be drilled, and it is equally obvious that in certain rare cases—of which Hardknot is one—no natural piece of ground in the neighbourhood could be used for this purpose. It is common to find a paved area just outside a fort

ROMAN ESKDALE

(e.g., Slack, Gellygaer, Ambleside, etc.), and another Cumberland fort, Maryport, has a levelled area not unlike that at Hardknot, a little distance away, commanded by an artificial mound. These remains at Maryport, however, have recently been destroyed by the building of new houses. The artificial mound is no doubt the TRIBUNAL, the place from which the commanding officer addressed his troops and watched them on parade.

What sights have been seen from the summit of this stony knoll ? What feet have rested upon it ? Did an Emperor of Rome once stand here, his scarlet cloak flapping in the wind, his glittering staff-officers to right and left, while the motionless ranks below listened to their Cæsar, the eccentric genius with the philosopher's beard and the long inquiring nose, telling them of the great Wall whose course he had but now marked out on the ground, and whose plans he signed last week ? Can we catch a few of his words, borne by the wind to where we crouch behind a rock ? . . . He has ordained a vast number of forts scattered over Britain, and a great barrier crossing the island from sea to sea ; he reviews his armies and commends their loyalty, their courage and discipline ; stern necessity has forbidden them to conquer the whole world, but they have conserved the frontiers of the Empire and made them safe for ever. . . The dream fades and the broken words come before our eyes as they stand cut on those crumbling stones—one now in Newcastle, one in London—that once bore the text of Hadrian's address to his army in Britain.

ROMAN ESKDALE

HARDKNOT CASTLE : ITS HISTORY

No ancient writer mentions Hardknot Castle ; no inscriptions (apart from one unintelligible fragment) have been found there ; and we do not know either its ancient name or what regiment lay in garrison there. But we can say something of its history. That is because we can argue by analogies: we can say that certain types of building belong in general to certain periods, and that certain fashions in perishable things such as pottery lasted for a certain length of time. This method of reconstructing history from archæological data has made great strides within living memory, and upon this method everything that can be said about Hardknot depends.

This is not the place for a discussion of the evidence. It has been worked out along four different lines : first, by general probabilities based on what we know of other Roman sites in the district, notably Ambleside; secondly, by the resemblance of Hardknot Castle, in lay-out and construction, to other forts that can be dated with accuracy ; thirdly, by the coins found in it ; and fourthly, by the pottery. The first line of argument is inconclusive. It takes us no further than the probability that Hardknot belongs to the late first or early second century. The second line is more profitable. It brings Hardknot into close connexion with a series of forts built about the beginning of Trajan's reign—say, in the first ten years of the second century. The third line suggests an occupation mainly confined to the reign of Trajan. The fourth is by far the most explicit and reliable. It proves quite certainly that Hardknot was occupied, roughly speaking, for the first quarter of the second century.

ROMAN ESKDALE

A close study of this evidence in all its bearings has made it probable that the fort was originally built about A.D. 100 or soon afterwards—not later than A.D. 110. During this period there is reason to believe that a certain amount of work was being done in Britain by way of increasing the defensive strength of the Roman position in the north. The Wall had not yet been built or dreamed of, but the desirability of a proper system of fortifications was already being felt, and it seems that about A.D. 103 a certain number of old forts, hitherto made of wood and earth, were rebuilt in stone, and a certain number of new ones built in the same material. Hardknot falls into this group of Trajanic forts.

The reason for its foundation is not hard to guess. Agricola, when he built the road from Lancaster to the Irish Sea, placed a fort at Kendal, another at Ambleside, and another at Ravenglass. Now the distance from Ambleside to Ravenglass was about 20 miles, over two high mountain passes ; and Ravenglass may have been thought dangerously exposed to raids from the sea, especially as there was no other Roman fort on the Cumberland coast, so far as we know, and the Irish may already have begun to develop the piratical habits for which they became famous two or three centuries later. In these circumstances it was a reasonable move to give up the fort at Ambleside—excavation there suggests that the early fort was not occupied very long—and replace it with a fort at Hardknot, within easy reach of Ravenglass. Even so, the distance between the new fort and Kendal was not excessive. From Kendal to Ravenglass is about 33 miles ; Ambleside divides this distance into 13 and 20, Hardknot into 24 and 9. This alteration, which

ROMAN ESKDALE

would have been a mistake if there had been any danger from the hill-dwellers of the Lake District, would be wise if the sea was the chief seat of peril.

The pottery makes it clear that a full garrison, a cohort of auxiliaries, lay at Hardknot for a considerable time. The date of evacuation can be fixed at about A.D. 130. This date falls midway between two important events. In A.D. 122 Hadrian came to Britain and set on foot the building of the great Wall, which was completed by, at latest, A.D. 127. It would be easy to understand why a fort like Hardknot might be abandoned when the Wall was built, for that would demand a complete reorganisation of the frontier defences and a considerable redistribution of troops. But Hardknot seems to have survived the building of the Wall. In A.D 142 it was resolved to move the frontier forward from the Newcastle—Carlisle line to a line between Glasgow and Edinburgh. This, with the building of the Antonine Wall between the Forth and Clyde, involved another shuffling of garrisons, and in particular a withdrawal of troops from Wales. But this does not seem to have been the occasion of the evacuation of Hardknot, for Hardknot seems to have been abandoned before it came about.

A fort abandoned by its garrison was not necessarily left quite deserted. In many such cases we have evidence that a caretaker was left in charge, and some part of the fort buildings might be converted into a rest-house or inn for people passing along the road. This certainly happened at Hardknot. We have already seen that certain alterations were made in the bath-house, making it less suitable for a regimental bath and club, but more suitable for a wayside rest-house ; and here, we may suppose,

ROMAN ESKDALE

a caretaker lived and gave shelter and food to passers-by, at any rate people passing by on official business. That there was ever a great deal of traffic is very unlikely. We cannot suppose that traders and travellers used the road to any considerable extent. There are no remains along its course such as to suggest that it connected centres of population between which trade would pass. If goods came to Ravenglass by sea, they would not travel by road to the neighbourhood of Kendal; it would be easier to ship them in the first instance to the ports of Morecambe Bay. For 250 years after the evacuation of Hardknot we must think of this mountain road looking very much as it looks to-day, except that, instead of holiday-makers, we must imagine an occasional imperial messenger, a convoy of military stores, or a draft of recruits for the fort at Ravenglass, resting at the bath-house while the caretaker brings out refreshments, and listening to the croak of the ravens and the low roar of Hardknot Gill.

THE ROMAN FORT AT RAVENGLASS

Except for a small portion lying between the railway and the shore, the whole of the Roman site at Ravenglass is situated in the private grounds of Walls house, which belongs to the Muncaster Castle estate, and is in the hands of a private tenant. Readers wishing to visit the site will remember that they are the guests of the tenant, and that if some people wander about the grounds without asking permission, others may find themselves unable to obtain it.

The fort, compared with Hardknot Castle, is not easy to find. If you enter the gateway and walk along the drive leading southwards to Walls, you

ROMAN ESKDALE

come to a ruined house standing on your left. That is the bath-house of the Roman fort. Go past it and walk on another 30 yards, and then turn to your right. The outer ditch of the fort is just in front of your feet. Ten yards in front of you is the inner ditch. Twenty yards in front of you is the rounded north-east corner of the fort. The drive, from this point until it curves round in front of the house, runs parallel to the east side of the fort, along the lip of its outer ditch. All along this east side the rampart is very clear, forming a mound about 5 feet high and 140 yards long in a straight line through the shrubbery. Beside it runs a well-marked ditch, and a second ditch is less clear but obvious enough.

Going west from the north-east corner towards the sea, the north side of the fort is visible as a sharp escarpment, falling away into a rather deep ditch, for 60 yards. Here it is interrupted by the railway, which has been driven obliquely through the fort in a cutting, entering at the south-west corner and coming out in the middle of the north side. If you cross the railway you can find the northern edge of the fort going on in the same straight line on the other side of the cutting, but very soon rounded off by the erosion of the sea.

Along the south side the rampart of the fort is clearly visible, beginning close to Walls house and running westward in the form of a rounded bank, about 112 yards long, until it is destroyed by the railway cutting. South of this bank there may have been a ditch, but it is not now visible; there is a narrow flat shelf of ground, with a modern drive running along it, bounded by the fort on the north and a ravine on the south.

ROMAN ESKDALE

The seaward rampart of the fort has disappeared ; the sea, eroding the low bluff on which it stood, has washed it away, and now one can see, close to the summit of this bluff, layers of discoloured soil containing pottery, tiles, and charcoal, showing the level of the Roman floors.

So far as can now be seen, the fort measured about 140 yards square, which would make it rather over $3\frac{1}{2}$ acres in area inside the defences. It doubtless had gates, corner towers and internal buildings a good deal like those of Hardknot ; but of them we know nothing definite. No traces of them can now be seen on the ground, and when some digging was done in 1886 it was found that the buildings of the fort had been very thoroughly ruined by persons searching for stone, and, this being so, excavations were stopped. None the less, it would be well worth while to dig here again, because we know a great deal more than we did in 1886 about getting solid scientific results out of disturbed and plundered sites. The real trouble about the work done in those days was that people did not watch the men digging ; they set them to work and left them to it, so that there was no possibility of discovering anything except what was obvious to a perfectly untrained and uneducated mind. On this particular occasion, for instance, the men found an inscribed stone, but threw it into the sea because the letters on it were " English letters," so they knew it could not be of any value !

The only recorded discovery in the fort was made in 1850 during the construction of the railway. The men making the cutting through the fort came upon three underground chambers, 15 feet deep, more or less pyramidal in shape, 10 or 12

ROMAN ESKDALE

feet square at the bottom, which was flagged, and narrowing as they ascended until they terminated in a square opening with a stone slab over it, two feet below the present surface. The sides were made of tree-trunks laid horizontally.

We know of various kinds of underground chambers in Roman forts. There are hypocaust-chambers, but these are shallow and wide. There are rubbish-pits, but these are mere holes, not carefully lined and paved. There are wells, but these do not spread out into large flagged chambers. And there are dug-outs or sunk dwellings in which men lived, but these are not approached through a narrow hole which would make ventilation and lighting impossible. But there are also storage-chambers, which are often vaulted and paved, and there can be little doubt that this is the explanation of the cellars found at Ravenglass. They would serve for the storage of wheat and other things, and a seaport like Ravenglass is a natural place in which to find such additional facilities for storing goods brought, perhaps, by sea.

Outside a Roman fort there was always a village of some kind where friends and relations of the soldiers could live. The soldiers were allowed to marry, though their marriages were not legally recognised until they had completed their 25 years' service and had been given their " honourable discharge " and elevated to the rank of Roman Citizen ; but these unofficial marriages were, it seems, binding in actual custom ; and the result was that a great many of the soldiers, though living in barracks inside the fort, kept a wife and family in the village outside. Then there would be shops of various kinds ; temples where the men could indulge

ROMAN ESKDALE

their sometimes recondite and eccentric religious tastes (for a half-civilised auxiliary was not likely to feel that he had altogether settled his accounts with heaven when he had joined in the official regimental worship of Jupiter and the divine Emperor) ; taverns where they could get something to eat and drink more interesting than what was going in barracks ; and, as the centre of all this lighter side of garrison life, the regimental bath-house acting as a club where the men could play games and spend their spare time, on wet days, in warmth and comfort. As time went on, the barracks gradually became less important and the village more so. The Emperor Severus allowed men to live permanently outside the fort with their families ; and his son, Caracalla, in A.D. 212, extended the Roman Citizenship to all inhabitants of the Empire, so that the right to contract a legal marriage, instead of being conferred on auxiliary soldiers at their discharge, belonged to them by birth. The garrison in a fort like this was turning by degrees into a soldier-peasantry, settled on the land and reluctant to move far from its home village. By the fourth century it had become a peasant militia.

The whole of this must apply to the history of Roman Ravenglass. North of the fort is an area of some three or four acres, all littered with Roman pottery and relics of occupation. This is the site of the civil settlement. No foundations are traceable on the surface, and the houses here were mostly, no doubt, huts of a simple and primitive kind. But it is clear that there was a village of considerable size on the north side of the fort, and perhaps on the other sides also.

WALLS CASTLE: General View.

ROMAN ESKDALE

"WALLS CASTLE" : THE ROMAN BATH-HOUSE AT RAVENGLASS

The ruined building, locally known as Walls Castle, which stands beside the drive of Walls house, has been already mentioned. It stands about 40 yards from the north-east corner of the fort, and is the only striking relic visible on the site of Roman Ravenglass.

Walls Castle is the best preserved Roman building in the north of England. Nowhere else in the north—perhaps nowhere else in the whole country —is there a Roman house still standing to the full height of its walls. No other northern building even approaches it in this respect. The bath-house of the fort at Chesters, beside the North Tyne, falls far short of it in height, though it has many more rooms.

The remains now standing above ground form an irregular block about 50 feet long by 40 feet wide, consisting of two rooms and various projecting fragments of wall. One room is 15 ft. 11 in. by 14 ft. 7 in., the other 18 ft. 9 in. by 14 ft. 5 in. The two corners pointing towards the west and south seem to be true external angles, but everywhere else there are walls ending where they have been broken off, their continuation lost. The building is made of good red freestone, regularly coursed, with very hard mortar, and internally at least the walls are rendered with pink cement; their height is 12 ft. 6 inches. The doorways have relieving arches 9 feet from the ground, with lintels below, nicked to receive timber door-frames. There are traces of 5 windows with sills 4 feet from the ground; like most Roman windows, they are

ROMAN ESKDALE

heavily splayed internally. Most if not all of them have been reduced in size by blocking up their lower parts. In one place there is a semi-cylindrical round-headed niche, 3 ft. 6 in. high, 2 ft. 10½ in. broad, and 1 ft. 6 in. deep.

In 1881 some digging was done in order to recover the plan of the missing portion. It was found that the walls extended a considerable distance to the east, making the block altogether 90 feet long. East of the larger room (the one with

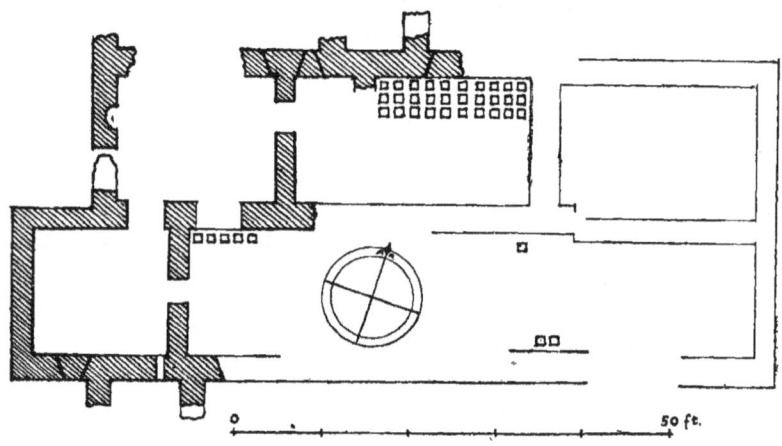

"WALLS CASTLE": ROMAN BATH-HOUSE, RAVENGLASS.

the niche), which seems to have had a solid floor, was a small room 15 ft. by 7 ft. 2 in., and then a room about 15 ft. square, with a hypocaust; beyond that was another larger room. The smaller of the two rooms now standing had a solid floor, but had once had a hypocaust, for an arch below ground-level led through its south wall into what had once, no doubt, been a furnace. East of this was a very long room with hypocaust heating, which may have

ROMAN ESKDALE

been subdivided by cross-walls which the excavators did not find. To northward and southward they did not try to complete the plan.

This, clearly, is a larger and more complicated bath-house than the little establishment at Hardknot. And, until the complete plan is discovered by further excavation, we cannot say with certainty how the various rooms were used. It looks as if the room with the niche were an entrance-hall or dressing-room, and the niche very likely contained a statue of Fortune ; but this is guessing.

THE HISTORY OF ROMAN RAVENGLASS.

We have already described the coming of the Romans to Ravenglass, and shown how they were led to choose this fine harbour as a naval base for their projected invasion of Ireland. To this theory of its origin we may add a theory as to its ancient name. In the official road-book of the Roman Empire, the " Antonine Itinerary " or Road-Book of the Emperor Antoninus (we do not know which of the many Emperors of that name) there is a road, the Tenth British Route, that leads from Cheshire through Lancashire and so to some places—Alone, Galava, Clanoventa—whose identity has long been a matter of doubt and controversy. Out of the controversy one fairly definite result has emerged : namely that there is a possibility, amounting to probability, that Alone is Kendal, Galava Ambleside, and Clanoventa Ravenglass. All other identifications are subject to fatal objections, demanding roads where no roads exist or forts where none are to be found : this alone fits the facts and therefore holds the field. And this theory mutually strengthens, and is strengthened by, the

ROMAN ESKDALE

theory that Ravenglass was Agricola's naval base for the invasion of Ireland. If that was its purpose, it must have been regarded as a place of some importance, and this would explain why the road leading to it was included in the Antonine road-book.

The ancient name of Ravenglass, then, was probably Clanoventa. That is not a Latin name, but a British one. The Romans hardly ever gave Latin names to the forts and towns which they built in outlying parts of their empire ; they almost always called them by native names. The element VENTA in Clanoventa is found elsewhere in, for instance, Venta Belgarum, " Venta of the Belgae," now Winchester, and it seems to mean " market." This suggests that there was already a sea-port at Ravenglass, used for purposes of local trade, before the Romans came.

A long time after it was first established, the fort here was garrisoned by the First Cohort of Morini. The Morini were a seafaring people living in the extreme north of France, round Calais and Boulogne. It is natural to suppose that they were placed here from the first, in order to use their seamanship (for they were a seafaring tribe) at a place where seamanship was required.

But it is possible that the earliest garrison at Ravenglass consisted not of Morini, but of Usipi from Germany. There is a dramatic story in Tacitus (AGRICOLA, chapter 28) of a cohort of Usipi which was sent to Britain in the year after that in which Agricola is said to have fortified the coast opposite Ireland. These raw barbarian levies were placed somewhere in a fort by the sea, with a centurion and some old soldiers to knock them into

WALLS CASTLE: Relieving Arch over Door
Photo by Miss M. C. Fair.

WALLS CASTLE: Niche
Photo by Miss M. C. Fair. To face P. 47.

ROMAN ESKDALE

shape. They mutinied, killed their taskmasters, and seized three ships, in which they set out for home. They did not know how to get there, but they knew that they must sail either round Cape Wrath or round Land's End. They chose the northern route, as it seems, and embarked on their adventurous voyage, landing from time to time to provision themselves, which they had to do by force, and were at last brought to such an extremity of want that they were compelled to cast lots to kill and eat some of themselves. But they succeeded in sailing round Britain and making their landfall on the Dutch or Frisian coast, only to lose their ships and to be arrested by the people as pirates. A few survivors, sold as slaves into Roman territory, told the story of their adventure.

We are not told where the fort was from which the Usipi sailed. But it must have been on the west coast, or they would not have had to sail round Britain ; and of the three or four possible sites, Ravenglass is the likeliest.

The fort was probably occupied throughout the Roman period. There is some reason to think that the garrison was not withdrawn until late in the fourth century, when the Wall was abandoned and the Roman troops confined to the south and east of Britain. After this it is natural to suppose that half-Romanized Britons continued for a long time to inhabit the village round the fort and perhaps the fort itself ; but of this we cannot be certain, and, since all the western coast of Britain was swept by Irish raiders in the fourth and fifth centuries, it is very possible that Clanoventa was ravaged and plundered out of existence. When the Norsemen settled along this coast in the tenth century they

ROMAN ESKDALE

called the Roman ruins " Mulcaster," the fort on the headland (MULI), corrupted later to Muncaster ; and one of the Celtic people who came with them, Glas by name, or " Grey," established himself close by at Renglas (the REIN or strip of Glas), now Ravenglass.

In the twelfth century we find the De Penningtons, lords of the manor of Ravenglass, living on the site of the Roman fort and actually, we are told, using the Roman bath-house as their dwelling before they moved to the site of Muncaster Castle. This adaptation as a medieval manor-house is a strange fate to befal a building eleven centuries old, which may have stood empty for between seven and eight hundred years ; and it is a testimony to the fact that a well-constructed building will defy the ravages of time and the buffetings of the weather almost indefinitely, until human hands deliberately destroy it.

Deserted once more, this ruin so worked on the imagination of its neighbours that strange stories began to be told of it. Writers of the late sixteenth and early seventeenth century identified it with the Lyons Garde of the Arthurian romances, the Castle Perilous beside the Island of Avilion, where dwelt the Lady of the Fountain ; or they said that it was the castle of King Eveling or Avalloc, the husband of the sea-fairy Morgan le Fay, who was king over the island in which lived the blessed dead.

And if you stand there as dusk is falling, and think of the place as it was before Walls house was built or its shrubberies planted ; when no railway ran through the ruined fort, and when the roofless building stood looking out over the sands and

ROMAN ESKDALE

shallows of the harbour ; it is not difficult to recapture the sense of a haunted spot, and to feel that some strange far-off life may yet cling to the stones that have stood for eighteen centuries where the Romans placed them. You may dismiss the fairy-tales of King Eveling and the Lady of the Fountain as idle superstitions ; but if you have eyes to see and ears to hear, ghosts will stand before you in the twilight, Roman soldiers and British women will move about the vanished village ; you shall hear Agricola's men discussing the invasion of Ireland, and see the Usipi launching their ships while the bodies of their officers lie mangled on the beach.

www.ingramcontent.com/pod-product-compliance
Lightning Source LLC
Chambersburg PA
CBHW022121090426
42743CB00008B/953